WTF

WHAT THE FORK?

an unpretentious guide to formal dining
for informal people

WHAT THE FORK?

an unpretentious guide to formal dining
for informal people

SUE JACQUES
THE CIVILITY CEO®

PALINDROME PUBLISHING COMPANY

DISCLAIMER

The purpose of this book is to educate and enlighten.

Though dining protocols have existed for centuries, advice may vary from circumstance to circumstance and consultant to consultant. This text is a general reference about formal dining. Every effort has been made to make this guide as accurate as possible. There may, however, be unintentional oversights. The author and Palindrome Publishing Company shall have neither liability nor responsibility to any person or entity with respect to loss or damage caused (or alleged to have been caused, directly or indirectly) by the information in this book. If detailed dining instruction is required, professional training should be sought.

Library and Archives Canada Cataloguing in Publication

Jacques, Sue, author
What the fork? : an unpretentious guide to formal dining
for informal people / Sue Jacques.

Issued in print and electronic formats.
ISBN 978-0-9920030-0-5 (pbk.).--ISBN 978-0-9920030-1-2 (pdf)

1. Table etiquette. I. Title.
BJ2041.J33 2013   395.5'4   C2013-906540-7
                                 C2013-906541-5

Cover, graphic, and text design: Erynn Lyster ~ Urban Motif Design Inc.
Editor: Barbara McNichol
Illustrations: Sean deLima
Photography: Jessica Jacques Nogueira | kidsphoto Canada

Special and corporate bulk purchase rates are available.
Please call 877.977.2702 for more information.

Sue Jacques ~ The Civility CEO® is available to speak at your live event.
Visit www.TheCivilityCEO.com to learn more.

Printed in Canada

Palindrome Publishing Company
Calgary, AB

For Liliana and Natalia,
the two sweetest choices on the menu of my life.

INTRODUCTION

"The world was my oyster, but I used the wrong fork.

Oscar Wilde

*W*E LIVE IN AN AGE OF McMANNERS. In our overscheduled lives, pre-packaged "convenience" foods have changed the way we dine. These days, a family meal might mean zipping through a drive-thru lane, supersizing our order, and eating out of a paper bag as we rush to yet another appointment, meeting, or practice.

I wasn't raised with a silver spoon in my mouth, and if you're reading this book, you probably weren't either. In fact, there was a time when I thought formal dining skills were reserved for mucky-mucks with highfalutin' jobs and sophisticated social lives.

In the casual, middle-class family I grew up in, our fanciest epicurean adventure was going to the local steakhouse, famous for its "All-you-can-eat!" salad bar. Or, we'd host a Sunday dinner or holiday feast. That's when the *good* dinnerware came out. We'd even unearth the cloth napkins!

> **From gracefully manipulating a simple pair of chopsticks to confidently navigating a complex plethora of silverware, I observed an elegance that my own dining style lacked.**

I first realized that knowing how to dine is a valuable skill in my early thirties when I took an extended solo journey to Europe, the Middle East, and Asia. I couldn't help but notice how the people I encountered in other cultures ate differently than I did. From gracefully manipulating a simple pair of chopsticks to confidently navigating a complex plethora of silverware, I observed an elegance that my own dining style lacked.

Having attended countless weddings, banquets, and conference dinners, I thought I could hold my own when it came to wielding a knife and fork. But I learned the hard way that knowing how to dine correctly *really* matters when a charming gentleman invited me to be his date at a black-tie dinner several years ago.

After I said yes, my priorities were buying the perfect dress, finding a pair of fabulous shoes, and making sure every hair was in place on the day of the event. Learning how to behave appropriately at such a high-caliber occasion never even occurred to me. I thought I knew all there was to know.

I didn't ask my date about the purpose of the event, and if he told me, I didn't pay attention. I was focused on the thrill of an invitation to a sparkly see-and-be-seen gala.

When we walked in the door of the ballroom, the glamour wowed me. Tuxedos and taffeta were in abundance. I had never attended anything like it in my life.

The maître d' led us to our seats at the center of the head table, which was on a riser at the front of the room. I noticed a row of formally clad waiters at full attention behind us, one server for each couple. You'd think I'd have caught on by this point that being seated at the head table was *special*, but I still didn't get it. I was too busy admiring the magnificence of the scene.

When dinner was served, it seemed odd to me that no one else in the room was eating. Instead, everyone looked at those of us seated at the head table. They smiled at me; I smiled back at them. They smiled more at me; I continued to smile at them. Then the waiter, of whom I could see no more than a white-gloved hand and a condensation-beaded silver water pitcher, leaned over my right shoulder and, pretending to fill my already full glass, whispered, "They're waiting for you to begin, Madam."

And that's when I looked at the place setting. Before me, I found a dizzying array of plates, glasses, and silverware—more than I owned! And it was in that moment, with all eyes on me, I realized I didn't have the slightest idea how to manage the meal before me. The phrase that went through my head sounded *something* like, "What the fork do I do now?"

So I did what most of us would do in that circumstance: I faked it. My gaze shifted from one side to the other as I watched what everyone else did, and somehow I got through the meal. As it turned out, the evening's event honored my escort for his volunteer work with a service agency—hence our placement at the center of the head table. Duh.

> *I still vividly recall how uncomfortable I felt that evening when I realized I didn't know how to dine with confidence and grace.*

That dinner occurred on a Saturday night. The following Monday morning I signed up for a dining etiquette class. To my surprise, I enjoyed it so much that I continued my etiquette education, culminating in certification as an etiquette and protocol consultant.

Ultimately I changed careers, transitioning from 18 years as a forensic death investigator at the medical examiner's office to become a professional speaker, business consultant, confidence coach, and writer. My expertise lies in corporate and medical civility, executive etiquette, personal branding, and professionalism. I feel blessed to have found a way to blend my unique experience with my education, passion, and skills. And my business has flourished.

Yet I still vividly recall how uncomfortable I felt that evening when I realized I didn't know how to dine with confidence and grace. If I can save one person the embarrassment I experienced, then this book has done its job.

You may never attend a soirée like the one I described, but it's likely you'll be invited to at least one formal dining event over the course of your life. It may be a wedding, a business meal, a date, a cruise, a job interview, or a dinner to meet your future in-laws for the first time (gulp!). No matter what the occasion, I sincerely hope that, after reading *What The Fork?,* no uncertainty passes through your mind when the pressure is on.

Oh, and that dashing man who invited me to be his date? We recently celebrated our 17th wedding anniversary!

Yours in civility,

Sue Jacques
The Civility CEO®

HOW TO USE THIS BOOK

"

Food is our common ground, a universal experience.

James Beard

"

HOUGH DINING PROTOCOLS have existed for centuries, they can vary from person to person, family to family, situation to situation, generation to generation, place to place, and culture to culture. Whether you're hosting a small dinner party and wondering how to set the table, or you're unsure how to tell someone next to you at a formal banquet that they have food between their teeth, the fundamentals of fine dining remain the same.

What The Fork? is a reliable, practical, and straight-forward reference guide for you. Through common language and a conversational tone, this book provides vital information about standard contemporary dining practices that you can use in a variety of professional and personal scenarios in Western society.

These pages contain the cardinal guidelines of formal dining. They reflect respect for the host, for yourself, and for other diners, as well for the people who prepare, serve, and clean up the meal. You'll even learn to respect the food itself! In fact, later in this book, you'll find out why something as simple as lettuce is worthy of respect.

The book features eight sections, organized in a way you can quickly and easily find what you're looking for. I recommend you begin by reading it from beginning to end to familiarize yourself with the nuances of formal dining. From there, you will know exactly where to turn to find the information you need in certain situations.

In addition to understanding what your responsibilities are as a host and as a guest, you will learn the value of knowing how to dine with elegance and poise. And as you will see, when it comes to business, the confidence you bring into the dining room is as at least as important as the confidence you show in the board room.

All of the tasks involved in preparing for a formal meal—from invitations to seating plans and RSVPs—are detailed in *What The Fork?* You'll find suggestions on whether and when to order alcohol, how to handle special dietary requirements, who pays for a meal, how much to tip, and what to do if you're invited to a private club.

An entire section is devoted to dining procedures, including napkin use, place settings, and some of the courses commonly offered at a formal meal. The two most common styles of dining—Continental and North American—are reviewed in detail.

The book addresses other specifics, like exchanging handshakes and business cards, making introductions, what to do with handbags, briefcases, and electronic devices, how to have appropriate conversations, and what to do when awkward situations arise. You will also learn whether personal grooming or wearing a hat is ever appropriate at the dining table, and how to follow up after a formal meal with graciousness and civility.

Though I cannot *guarantee* your success if you follow these tips, I sincerely hope they work as well for you as I have intended.

WTF? WHAT IS A WTF? BOX?

Throughout this book, you'll see WTF? boxes, like this one. In them you'll find the most common Corporate Conundrums™ and social stumbling blocks I've encountered over the years. Be sure you take note of them!

Remember, this book highlights the *basics* of formal dining. It is designed for ordinary people who live normal, busy lives—as you do—who may never have had the opportunity, desire, or need to learn about crystal, china, linen, and silverware. But one day, when you least expect it, you'll receive an elegant invitation to a formal dinner and realize that manners *really do* matter.

I may not have known what to do way back when, but now *you* will!

WTF

PART ONE

WHY DO THESE THINGS MATTER?

"

One of the very nicest things about life is the way we must regularly stop whatever it is we are doing and devote our attention to eating.

Luciano Pavarotti

"

⌒ WHY DO THESE THINGS MATTER?

*B*ELIEVE IT OR NOT, your behavior during a meal can affect your job, your relationships, and your success. If you blow your nose in the linen napkin, talk with your mouth full, lick your knife, or check your smartphone every 10 seconds, there's a good chance you're irritating other people. The thing is, most people won't tell you if you have annoying dining habits, even when they feel terribly uncomfortable with your actions.

The onus is on *you* to know whether or not your conduct is appropriate. And that can be hard to ascertain when you've either grown up with, adopted, or are surrounded by an overly casual attitude. Why? Because indifference about your behavior—at the dining table and beyond—can have a negative impact on your personal and professional relationships.

I've coined a word to describe our increasingly civility-starved society: *mannerexia*. It represents the atrophy of our culture's overall appetite for formality. This malady can be remedied with a dose of Civility CPR; an injection of Courtesy, Professionalism, and Respect—at home, at work, and in our communities.

And it all begins with an activity as simple as sitting down to eat.

> *The thing is, most people won't tell you if you have annoying dining habits, even when they feel terribly uncomfortable with your actions.*

BUSINESS DINING

Professionalism extends far beyond the board room. Executives I've worked with have told me they expect their managers, salespeople, and team leaders to socialize, entertain, and dine with as much competence as they use to negotiate multimillion-dollar deals.

That's easier said than done, though, because proper dining skills are seldom taught in business school—or grade school, for that matter. Having an education doesn't mean having table manners. I was once seated next to a professional engineer at a business lunch and saw him pick up and eat his prime rib *with his hands*. Thankfully, he used a fork for his gravy-soaked mashed potatoes!

Having solid dining skills may even land you that plum job. Often, employers invite prospective employees to join them for a meal to see how comfortable they are when there's both money *and* food on the table. Which is why dining finesse should be standard in every businessperson's toolkit. And that can't be acquired by osmosis; it takes practice to eat and entertain with ease. As many deals are sealed in the dining room as in the board room. Never make the mistake of thinking that your table manners are unimportant.

> *... there is more to learn about dining than how to hold a knife and fork.*

Companies around the world rely on employees to represent their corporate brand with confidence, including during a business meal. But there's more to learn about dining than how to hold a fork and knife. You also need to understand your responsibilities as a host or guest, when to bring up the topic of business, where to seat people, how to handle the bill, and more. These lessons carry as much importance as what you should do with your tableware.

DINING SOCIALLY

Human beings have gathered around food from the beginning of time. Meals are reasons to visit, celebrate, and confer. Whether at a casual sports gathering or an elaborate wedding reception, people are still expected to follow a basic set of rules when they come together to eat.

Passing food politely, carrying on respectful conversations, and maintaining decorum have always made dining together enjoyable and memorable. That continues to be true, even in today's fast-paced age of abbreviated courtesy.

But the frenetic style of life these days makes it increasingly rare for families to enjoy regular sit-down meals together. As a result, many children never participate in leisurely meals that are uninterrupted by electronics or other distractions. They often don't get involved in ritual tasks such as setting and clearing the table or participating in meaningful discussions. It's natural, then, that as these children become adults, they feel uncomfortable in more formal settings.

I recall being seated in a restaurant next to a table of 20-somethings who were having a lively debate about which bread plate belonged to whom. Arguments for the right-sided plate were countered with logic for the one on the left. They eventually got so hungry during the discourse that one bold young man finally spoke up and declared his was the one with the biggest dinner roll on it. I'm pleased to report he chose the correct plate—the left-sided one! But in all fairness, there's no way to know these dining details unless they are taught.

> **Whether at a casual sports gathering or an elaborate wedding reception, people are still expected to follow a basic set of rules when they come together to eat.**

Another time, an awards dinner I attended featured a lovely five-course meal. When a serving of fruity sorbet arrived as a palate cleanser, the man seated next to me exclaimed, "Dessert? We haven't even had a proper dinner yet!" He didn't understand that the tasty refreshment was meant to neutralize his taste buds after the salad course in preparation for the entrée. And he wasn't alone. In fact, before I learned the intricacies of formal dining, I might have blurted out the same thing!

CULTURAL VARIATIONS

Dining practices vary around the world. When traveling, we owe it to the people whose cultures we visit to demonstrate respectful behavior while we're there. Of course, that includes learning about different dining styles as well as understanding the expectations of the hosts and other guests.

It's always advisable to research local customs for your destination before a journey so you can prepare for the subtleties within the societies you will encounter. You'll find that people from all walks of life appreciate the efforts of someone who asks questions, is open to fresh experiences, and enjoys new flavors, foods, and festivities.

You don't have to travel to discover these differences, though. Even at home we encounter a variety of diverse cultures. Dining in ethnic restaurants is a wonderful way to learn about the traditions of people from distant places. In fact, the proprietors, chefs, and servers at these establishments are usually more than happy to share stories and details about their homelands. Ask away!

Keep in mind that not everyone may understand the local customs where *you* live or work. For example, I know a group of people who gathered for cocktails after work on a Friday afternoon. Their newest colleague had recently arrived from another country. He excitedly brought a fully cooked chicken to the pub and placed it in the middle of the table. According to his customs at home, it was considered polite to bring such an offering of food to share with a group. Unfortunately, his misunderstood generosity ended in an embarrassing situation for him, his associates, and the pub's manager, who had to ask the man to take his chicken elsewhere.

I encourage you to warmly welcome people from other cultures who have moved to your community or joined your place of work. You could simply introduce yourself, invite them for a visit, or prepare and deliver a small gift basket. Be sure to share information about some of the surrounding amenities, neighborhood or office highlights, and maybe even your contact information in case they ever have any questions or need help. It is generous and thoughtful to help newcomers navigate local—and often unfamiliar—customs.

The bottom line is this: at home, at work, in your community, and wherever your journey takes you, exhibiting respectful and mannerly behavior has a positive impact on the relationships you develop.

WTF

PART TWO

MEETING PEOPLE AND MAKING INTRODUCTIONS

"

Communication is key. How you introduce yourself is very important. Practice makes perfect.

Ken, from the movie Toy Story 3

MEETING PEOPLE AND MAKING INTRODUCTIONS

*W*E ALL KNOW what it feels like when introductions aren't made. We end up awkwardly looking at each other and wondering what to say. This often happens when we forget someone's name or they forget ours, and can be especially uncomfortable in professional situations. In the business world, the way you introduce yourself and others can make or break your relationships.

The anatomy of an introduction

A good introduction consists of 5 Ps: *Preparation* (knowing who's who), *Precedence* (understanding where people stand in the hierarchy), *Pattern* (establishing a consistent technique), *Pronunciation* (saying names clearly and correctly), and *Parallels* (adding a point of commonality).

It is important that you feel comfortable introducing yourself and others, even at a business meal. Introductions begin as soon as you approach the table.

If the people gathered are new to you, introduce your-self and anyone else who is with you. Rather than reach across the table to shake hands, go around to each person and offer your handshake while you say your name. As new people join your group, stand and introduce yourself to them whenever possible.

Never presume that people you've met before remember your name (and don't take it personally if they forget it!). Just go ahead and introduce yourself, and if time permits, include a statement about your relationship to the host, where you work, or what brings you to the occasion.

Protocols

Be aware of protocols when making formal introductions. In business, for example, you always say the name of the person who holds the most senior position *first* and then introduce other people *to* them, like this: "Jennifer, I'd like to introduce our regional branch manager, Todd Nordly, to you. Todd, this is our CEO, Jennifer Pommat." Note that the CEO's name is spoken first in this circumstance.

If you use the surname of one person, remember to use the surname of the other person, too. And most important, know that a client *always* holds the position of highest seniority, superseding even the CEO. So when a client is part of your group, be sure to say his or her name *first*, like this: "Carol, I'd like to introduce our CEO Jennifer Pommat to you. Jennifer, this is Carol Starling, our new client."

In social settings, it is common to introduce people slightly differently than you would in business. Rather than refer to their rank or corporate position, consider their seniority and gender. This means that in mixed company, you would say the name of the most senior woman in the group first, and then introduce other people *to* her, like this: "Aunt Donna, this is my friend Debbie. We used to work together." If no women are present, say the name of the eldest gentleman and introduce others to him.

> *Never presume that people you've met before remember your name (and don't take it personally if they forget it!).*

When you are making a formal introduction and one of the people has an honorific (Dr., Judge, Professor), make sure you address them by that title. They will let others know if they prefer to be called by their given name. Say the first and last name of the untitled person, too, like this: "Dr. Jones, I'd like to introduce Gordon Smith, a member of my sales team. Gordon, this is Dr. Samantha Jones, my dentist."

In very formal circumstances and for seniors, include titles for both people: "Judge Harrison, I'd like to introduce Mrs. Baker."

It is fine to ask your titled associate or friend how he or she prefers to be introduced. Some people would rather their honorific not be used or will immediately reply, "Please, call me Samantha." If you are the one who is introduced to Judge Harrison, Dr. Jones, or Mrs. Baker don't call them by their first name unless they invite you to do so.

> *Whenever you make an introduction, it's helpful to include something interesting about people to promote conversation.*

If you are meeting people in a receiving line, such as at a wedding or funeral, keep your interaction sincere and succinct so you don't hold things up. If someone doesn't know who you are, say your name, what your relationship is to the couple or the deceased, and introduce anyone who is with you. Briefly express your well wishes about the marriage or your condolences about the death (don't mix those up!), and keep on moving.

Whenever you make an introduction, it's helpful to include something interesting about people to promote conversation, such as, "Steve lives next door to us at the cabin," or, "Just like you, Kasey is an avid golfer."

If you ever need to introduce someone who used to be in your personal or professional circle but no longer is (like a person you used to date, work with, or be married to), it's thoughtful to use the word "former" rather than "ex" when referring to him or her.

Handling forgotten names

Most of us struggle to remember names, even of people we've met before. When this happens to you, acknowledge that you remember them and admit you've forgotten their name. If you recall something about the last time you met, like what event it was at or a story they shared with you, bring it up as evidence that it's not *them* you've forgotten; it's only their name.

This happened to me recently when I ran into someone I'd met very briefly over a year ago. For the life of me, I couldn't remember her name, yet I recalled every detail of our previous conversation. So I said, "Hi, I'm Sue. We met at this event last year. I remember you told me you were thinking about retiring from your position as a flight attendant with American Airlines, but somehow I've forgotten your name. Can you please remind me what it is? And tell me, what's happened since then?"

We all have personal boundaries, and many people feel uncomfortable with intimate greetings such as hugging and kissing. For some, these public displays of affection invade their physical space, particularly at work. Many others, however, feel like they haven't said a proper hello if there's been no warm embrace!

One's comfort level with hugging and kissing can be traced back to a variety of factors, including their family dynamics and cultural traditions, their natural level of empathy, what they've been taught as "appropriate" behavior, and the lingering results of any trauma they may have experienced, to name just a few.

Hugging

In this world, there are *huggers* and there are *trees*. Huggers are those who enjoy the feeling that comes with wrapping their arms around people and holding them close. For them, every greeting is a grasp. Trees, on the other hand, feel terribly uncomfortable with that level of physicality and can even feel trapped when in the arms of a hugger.

In a room full of people, you can usually spot the trees; they're the ones standing stiff and still, trying to figure out what on earth to do with their arms in the throes of an embrace from a hugger. You'll often notice that trees place their hands on huggers' shoulders in a feeble—and often uncontrollable—attempt to push the other person away and establish personal limits.

Be respectful of other people's private boundaries; don't just barrel in with a big hug when you meet someone, especially in business. When you're not sure about another person's feelings regarding hugging, you can simply ask, "May I give you a hug?"

> *Sometimes, no matter how well you get to know someone, a hug will never feel right. And that's okay. Just remember this: Before you embrace, give 'em some space.*

If you are greeting a group and want to hug one person and not the others, what should you do? I suggest you begin by offering a round of handshakes. Take a moment to get the lay of the land. Often, once a relationship has been established, that handshake will naturally lead to a hug. But sometimes, no matter how well you get to know someone, a hug will never feel right. And that's okay. Just remember this: *Before you embrace, give 'em some space.*

Kissing

In many cultures cheek kissing is a normal and expected greeting. This isn't about locking lips! The kind of kissing I'm referring to is when you greet one another by gently touching cheek to cheek, or, sometimes, lip to cheek. The number of pecks can vary from two to four, depending on where you are or where the other person is from. Keep in mind that this greeting—which is common in much of Europe, French-speaking Canada, the Middle East, the Mediterranean, and some Latin countries—is accepted among family members, friends, male and female colleagues, and acquaintances. One of the many beauties of our rapidly changing global landscape is that this greeting is becoming more standard in personal and professional interactions around the world. I remember learning this skill during my early travels, and I'm so glad I did!

These exchanges usually begin with a handshake, which is followed by one or both parties drawing the other closer. The left hand is then placed on the other person's right shoulder, and the cheek kissing follows (you normally alternate cheeks, right to left, but not always). Rather than beginning with a handshake, often the ritual starts with a gentle hug. If you don't know what to do, let the other person guide the greeting. Should you be traveling or meeting people from afar, find out ahead of time what the customary greeting is. There's no need to recoil from or resist a cheek kiss; it is a lovely way to say hello … and goodbye. Just be sure you've gotten to know someone a bit before greeting that person with such gusto!

Limp noodle. Dead fish. Bone crusher. These are just three common terms used to describe the less-than-stellar handshakes we've all exchanged at some point in our lives. You know what it feels like to be on the *receiving* end of one of these handshakes, but how do you know if you're the person *offering* them?

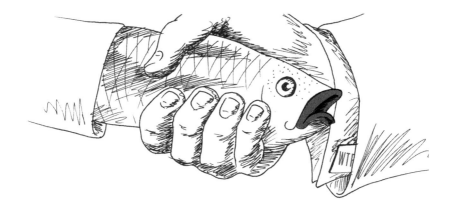

The all-too-common "Dead Fish" handshake. What's yours like?

My research shows that most people have never actually been taught how to shake hands. It's also true that the vast majority of people whose palms you press will never tell you outright if your handshake makes them cringe. Instead, they silently wince, flinch, or cower. And while it's good to be mindful of the many cultural, medical, religious, and psychological reasons behind the quality of someone else's handshake (or lack thereof), it's equally important to recognize how others are receiving yours.

WTF? HOW DO YOU TELL IF YOUR HANDSHAKE IS RESPECTFUL OR REPELLENT?

Here are six steps to save you the worry of wondering how your handshake measures up.

Don't wait: Today's North American culture is increasingly equal in terms of gender, age, and seniority—especially in business. Men don't need to wait for a woman to extend her hand first; nor do women need to wait for a gentleman to take the lead. In fact, you will exude confidence by extending your hand without hesitation to everyone you meet.

Stand up and look 'em in the eye: A handshake is considered a formal social greeting as well as an indication of sealing a deal, agreeing to disagree, or parting company. For those reasons, it's advisable to stand and make eye contact when you're about to shake hands. In most cultures (but not all), doing so shows respect.

Avoid obstacles: When accepting someone's outstretched hand, it's best to make sure there are no physical objects between you and the other person. In a restaurant or dining room, this might mean stepping around a table or chair to greet someone.

Start a webcast: Both feeble and fierce handgrips often simply result from physically misplacing the hand. To avoid unintentionally dainty or death-like grips, make sure that the web between the

thumb and index finger on your right hand meets the same web on the other person's right hand before you confidently grasp your fingers around the back of his or her palm.

Shake it up: *Offer a firm and crisp handshake, which has a beginning and an end. Two or three pumps originating from the elbow rather than the wrist is about perfect. Any more than that can be considered lingering, and one single shake can seem curt rather than courteous. Again, be mindful that people from other cultures or mindsets may offer you a different handshake—or none at all.*

Just say no: *Whether you're sick, injured, or just plain grossed out by shaking hands, you can still be diplomatic and professional when meeting others. Illness, for example, is a prime reason to decline a handshake. Rather than risk sharing your germs, you can say, "I'm feeling a little under the weather today. May I offer you my card instead of a handshake?"*

If you're not sure how your handshake feels to other people, it's okay to ask a trusted friend, family member, or colleague to evaluate it. The quality of your handshake can make or break your success.

EXCHANGING BUSINESS CARDS

Carry business cards with you to all professional and social events. You never know who you might meet and where you might meet them, and you don't want to be caught unprepared. I've been asked for my card countless times on airplanes, at cocktail parties, and even at the gym!

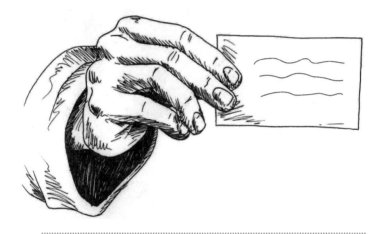

When presenting your card to someone, do so with the type facing them. Don't cover that precious information with your fingers.

In some cultures the presentation of a business card is a very formal ritual that includes using both hands and a slight bow. Find out what protocols are applicable if you are traveling or doing business with people from abroad.

When you receive someone's card, take a moment to look at it, and then make a verbal comment about it to help you remember that person.

Never deface someone else's card by writing on it. Instead, you may want to make notes about your interaction on a sticky note that you attach to the card when you're back at home or your office, or add appropriate comments to your contact list when transcribing that person's information to your computer or smartphone.

I recommend investing in a quality business card case so you can keep your cards clean, organized, and readily available, while keeping the cards you receive in pristine condition.

WTF? WHAT IF I DON'T WORK? DO I STILL NEED BUSINESS CARDS?

Whether or not you have a job, consider using a calling card for your social and private life. It's just like a business card, but with your personal contact information printed on it rather than your business contact information. If you're retired, between jobs, on leave, or going to school, it's advisable and convenient to present a suitable card to people you meet. Plus, if you work, you may not want to share your professional contact information with people you've met socially. It simply may not be appropriate for them to get in touch with you on company time. Calling cards are particularly handy for you or your family while traveling, because they provide a great way for people to contact you or stay in touch while you're away from work.

PART THREE

BEING A HOST AND BEING A GUEST

"

What is there more kindly than the feeling between host and guest?

Aeschylus

"

HETHER FOR BUSINESS or pleasure, you are equally as likely to take on the role of host as you are of guest at countless meals throughout your life. No matter which side of the table you're on, you must do more than just make an appearance and hope for the best. Here are some tips to help you prepare to entertain—and be entertained—with confidence and grace.

THE HOST

Hosting a meal requires much more effort than simply showing up. A host is responsible for extending the invitations, selecting the venue, making the reservation, confirming the details, pacing the meal, and paying the bill.

Skilled hosts know how to make introductions, generate interesting conversations, manage special dietary needs, deal with awkward situations, and make their guests feel welcome. They also understand where to seat people and how to dine with ease, knowing that guests rely on them to lead by example.

When inviting their guests, experienced hosts state the purpose and expected duration of the meal as well as relevant details including the location, parking options, contact phone numbers, and dress code. A tall order!

Sending invitations

The formality of an event generally dictates when and how invitations will be extended and the method of delivery.

As a rule of thumb, the more formal the event, the further in advance you will send invitations and the more traditional your delivery method will be.

Business and social meals for one-on-one or small get-togethers that will be hosted at your home or in a restaurant usually have a shorter lead-time and require less preparation than more elaborate events. That is why those invitations are often informal. Under these circumstances you may call, e-mail, or text your guest(s) and invite them to join you at a mutually convenient time and location. A formal RSVP is usually unnecessary; typically a verbal or electronic response is all that's required.

> *When inviting their guests, experienced hosts state the purpose and expected duration of the meal as well as relevant details including the location, parking options, contact phone numbers, and dress code. A tall order!*

Larger gatherings, both for business and social purposes, necessitate more detailed planning. Consequently, they also require more advance notice because of the amount of preparation that is required. Particulars such as selecting and reserving the appropriate venue and ordering an adequate amount of food and beverage can only be determined by knowing how many people will be in attendance. In these cases, simple pre-printed cards, group e-mails, or web-based invitations with automated RSVPs should be sent to the invitees.

For large or unique events such as global conferences, exclusive functions, surprise parties, weddings, and elaborate celebrations, hosts and event planners commonly send "Save the Date" notifications a few weeks or even months prior to the event so guests can schedule accordingly.

For highly formal or elite events, the invitations will likely be printed on quality paper and sent via courier or post, and will include an RSVP card for guests to complete and return.

Professionally designed event websites that accept electronic RSVPs are becoming increasingly popular, convenient, and acceptable for occasions of all types, including weddings, formal banquets, and corporate conferences.

No matter how you forward the invitation, just make sure it contains the necessary information that will help your guests make an informed decision about whether or not to attend the event.

WTF? WHAT DETAILS SHOULD BE ON AN INVITATION?

Here are 6 Ws to use as a guideline:

Who: *Specify exactly whom the invitation is meant for so guests aren't left wondering if they should attend alone or are welcome to invite their spouse, escort, children, or colleagues to accompany them.*

What: *Declare the purpose of the gathering so guests can prepare. If it's a birthday, wedding, or other celebration, clearly state specific requests such as "no gifts" or include details about a bridal or baby registry.*

When: *Include the beginning and ending time of the event, as well as what time speeches or entertainment will take place. Also be clear whether guests are welcome to arrive and leave during the event, such as for a "come and go" get-together.*

Where: *Share details about the venue, including the address, the name of the dining or meeting room, a contact phone number, and options for parking or alternate transportation.*

Wants: *Inquire if your guests have special dietary needs, food allergies, or other unique requests.*

Wear: *Be precise and straightforward about expected dress for the occasion. Stating something like "Executive Cocktail and Business Attire" is more descriptive than "Spiffy Casual" or "Contemporary Chic"—labels that lead to more questions than answers.*

Selecting a venue for smaller gatherings

When you invite people to join you for a meal in a restaurant, it's your duty to also choose the location—even if you are visiting a city other than your own. When you select a venue, consider the ambience, the menu choices, the location, and the amount of time you have.

It helps if you know your guests' particular likes, dislikes, or dietary requirements as well as how far they'll have to travel from their home, hotel, or office to reach the place you suggest. It is thoughtful to place their convenience over your own.

Also consider the purpose of the meal. What atmosphere will stimulate the discussion you wish to have? If you intend to engage in a private conversation, select a quiet restaurant with plenty of space between the tables. If you're looking for a more raucous celebration, you may want to choose an energetic café or bistro.

When extending the invitation, remember to share pertinent details with with your guests, including the address, exactly where you'll meet them, the dress requirements, and transportation or parking options. Also let them know how to contact you or the restaurant in case they need last-minute directions or are delayed.

Making seating arrangements

Whether you're in a small restaurant or a large ballroom, always offer your guests the seats with the best view.

Seat yourself with your back to that view—be it a picture window, a feature wall, or a piece of artwork—so your guests can enjoy the scenery. If you expect a speaker or entertainment during the meal, make sure your guests are positioned where they can clearly see the stage or podium.

> *It's also your job as host to be thoughtful about how you seat your guests in relation to each other.*

At a wedding, the bride and groom *are* the view. It is appropriate, then, to set up the room in such a way that guests can observe and appreciate the festivities as much as possible without craning their necks.

It's also your job as host to be thoughtful about how you seat your guests in relation to each other. Because you want to promote interesting conversation, you might pair people who share common interests or those from different backgrounds. It's usually acceptable to separate couples and seat them apart from one another if you like, especially if you think doing so will facilitate valuable interactions—or avert potential squabbling!

If you have a guest of honor at your table, always seat him or her to your (the host's) immediate right. If you host a meal as a couple, seat yourself at one end of the table with your spouse or partner at the opposite end (other than at your own wedding, of course!). If your guests of honor are another couple, seat one of them to the right of each of you, alternating men and women whenever possible.

If there is a head table, seat the guests of honor at the center of the head table facing other guests in the room.

Certain circumstances call for formal seating charts. Event and banquet planners are experts at determining who sits where. If you're organizing an occasion on your own, you can usually obtain a room configuration chart from the venue and use it to organize the seating. Or, you can access software programs or mobile applications to help you plan the seating. Your goal is to seat guests in pairs or groups that will encourage conversation and enhance their enjoyment.

Greeting guests

When you're hosting one or two people at a restaurant, let them know where you'll meet them (at the table, in the foyer, or outside the front door) and *be there first*. For gatherings of more than four or six people, whether a business meal with a group or a casual lunch with friends or family, you may take your seat when you arrive and ask the maître d' or waiter to show your guests to the table.

For even larger and more formal events—such as

corporate banquets, weddings, and award ceremonies—employ or recruit ample staff or volunteers to greet guests as they arrive. Instruct greeters to extend a warm welcome, answer questions, orientate guests to the venue's layout, and show people to their tables if they require assistance.

When you entertain in your home, it's equally imperative that guests be greeted, even for casual get-togethers. If you're too busy, ask someone to help you by answering the door, hanging coats, and bringing people together through conversation.

> *When a company hosts a large corporate event, it's advisable to seat at least one staff member at each table ... [to make] introductions and keeping dialogue flowing.*

Making people feel welcome
As a host, take the lead to make sure your guests are familiar with one another. At intimate gatherings, your role can be as simple as making verbal introductions and initiating conversations. The more people in attendance, the more helpful it is if you've prepared printed nametags or placeholders before the event.

When a company hosts a large corporate event, it's advisable to seat at least one staff member at each table. Ask that person to assume the responsibility of making introductions and keeping dialogue flowing. The same advice applies to social events, including weddings. In these cases you can ask friends or family members to oversee the discussions at their table, making sure that all guests are included. You may want to provide some background information about the other guests in advance so the table host can prepare.

Ordering meals

When there is no set menu, the host invites guests to order first. In some cases, it may be helpful to signal your guests to the appropriate price point for the occasion. You can make your companions feel comfortable by subtly guiding them with recommendations from the menu. You might say, for example, "They're known here for their filet mignon," indicating that it's okay for guests to order higher priced items.

When you are offering a set menu—as you would at a banquet, wedding, or conference—make sure to pre-select items that aren't messy and are easy for people to eat. Avoid dishes like ribs, long pasta, crab legs, or French onion soup, which can be difficult to consume with poise in a formal setting.

Handling special dietary requirements

If you know in advance that any of your guests have food

allergies or special dietary requirements, let the restaurant or caterer know as soon as possible. The people who prepare the meals need time to accommodate those kinds of requests. It is equally critical—and perfectly acceptable—to inquire ahead of time about your guests' requirements or restrictions when preparing to host a meal in your home.

Always take food allergies and sensitivities seriously; don't put even a drop of an ingredient in a dish that you're making when you know one of your guests may have a reaction to it. *You* may feel like you can't live without that dash of peanut oil or morsel of shellfish, but it could be fatal to someone else. In fact, it's best to change your menu altogether if it means ensuring someone's wellness.

Offering alcohol

No hard-and-fast rules exist about the appropriateness of serving alcohol. Many people observe cultural traditions or have personal principles or medical reasons for abstaining from ingesting alcohol, and some companies have detailed corporate policies on this topic. If you choose to offer alcohol and any of your guests decline, accept their position and move on. You do not need to ask for an explanation or needle them into joining you.

Here, use the same rule you would when ordering the meal: as host, invite your guest to order a drink first. If you're not offering alcohol, try saying something like, "Would you like a soft drink or coffee to start?" to ease any discomfort or confusion. When you are offering alcohol, you could say, "Would anyone care for a cocktail or glass of wine before dinner?" or, "I'm going to order a glass of wine. Would anyone care to join me?"

Always ensure that guests who imbibe have safe transportation home; drinking and driving is never an option.

Generating conversation

Implicit at any gathering over food is either a need or a desire for discussion. Barring the time when a guest speaker or entertainer may have the group's attention, the host has a duty to spark dialogue during the meal. It's important, then, for the host to feel confident in his or her own conversational skills.

Learning about guests ahead of time will help build that confidence. So will staying informed about current events, having interesting hobbies or stories to share, and asking thought-provoking questions. The best conversational skill a host can have is listening, because it honors guests by spotlighting the topics they find interesting.

At business meals, the host decides when it's appropriate to bring up "shop talk." It's helpful to have an agenda in mind that allows enough time to fully discuss each topic. There's not much point in commencing a complex conversation after dessert has been served and the meal is about to come to an end.

WTF? IS IT SUITABLE FOR THE HOST (OR SOMEONE THE HOST APPOINTS) TO SAY GRACE BEFORE A MEAL?

I get asked this a lot. The answer depends on a variety of factors. Consider these questions:

G = Gut

Do you think saying grace would make any of your guests feel uncomfortable?

R = Religion

Are most attendees of the same or similar faith?

A = Appropriateness

Are the purpose and place of the event conducive to a pre-meal blessing?

C = Courtesy

Are you offering grace as a show of respect for the attendees or guest(s) of honor?

E = Equality

Is the benediction general enough to include all cultures and spiritual beliefs?

If you are unsure, it's best to simply say a quiet prayer to yourself.

Dealing with complaints

Undercooked food, poor service, noisy neighbors, and uncomfortable discussions are just some of the myriad things that can go wrong during a meal. It's the host's job to deal with awkward situations or complaints diplomatically.

Be sure to check in with your guests periodically and ask if they're enjoying their meals. If any problems come up, tactfully bring them to the attention of the service staff to have them remedied. And I do mean tactfully. Some restaurant owners and staff have had it with disrespectful patrons. They're so tired of being treated poorly by diners that they've taken to expressing their disgruntlement online. Some have even been known to "out" latecomers, no-shows, and rude guests by name on Twitter, Facebook, or other social media sites.

As a host, pay attention to the conversations at the table and be prepared to intervene if you hear heated debates, unsuitable language, or confidential topics being discussed inappropriately. If you observe guests being obnoxious or out of line, take them aside and privately ask them to either modify their behavior or leave. If they're intoxicated, do whatever you must to see they get where they're going safely.

Paying the bill

With a couple of exceptions, the person who extends the invitation pays the bill. On some occasions, people agree in advance to pay for their own portion of the bill. On other occasions, your guests may not be in a position to accept complimentary meals or gifts because of their company's corporate guidelines or their personal preferences. Find out ahead of time.

When you're paying for a meal, you can clarify your

intention to treat someone by using the word "guest" in your invitation. For example, say, "Pat, I'd enjoy having you as my guest for lunch next week. It will give us a chance to review the final details of our project. Does next Tuesday at the new restaurant beside your office work for you?"

> *It is inappropriate to leave a meager or no tip. That money is usually shared with everyone involved in preparing your meal, from the person who peeled the potatoes to the one who cleared the dishes.*

As a host who's paying, it's preferable if the bill never comes to the table. Portable payment devices don't always make that easy, though. Here are three ways to see to this detail: (1) You can pre-arrange payment with your server before your guests arrive, (2) excuse yourself after the final course has been ordered to discreetly take care of the payment, or (3) stay behind to manage the transaction after seeing your guests to the door. Just let your waiter know in advance how you'd like to deal with the bill.

Be sure to add a tip for the service and effort you received. Standard gratuity in North American restaurants is 18–22 percent. It is inappropriate to leave a meager or no tip. That money is usually shared with everyone involved in preparing your meal, from the person who peeled the potatoes to the one who cleared the dishes. If you have an issue with your meal or the service, bring it to the attention of the server or headwaiter, who is in a position to make appropriate adjustments.

THE GUEST

It's a privilege to be invited to a meal, and whether the event is casual, formal, or grand, the guidelines remain the same. A gracious guest is one who respects the invitation and comes prepared to be engaging, conversational, and well mannered.

If you want to be a welcome guest, begin by dressing appropriately and arriving on time for the occasion. Be mindful of the behavior of the host; he or she is your guide. But, as is often the case, if your host's leadership or skills are lacking, it helps to have the confidence to know how to behave suitably.

I'll always remember the story someone told me about the CEO of his company inviting him and a few colleagues to share a celebratory evening meal at a posh restaurant. After ordering pre-dinner drinks, the CEO whipped out a cordless electric shaver from his breast pocket and took care of his five o'clock shadow *right at the table*! That's just one example of knowing when *not* to follow your host's lead!

Replying to RSVP requests

It's common to be asked to RSVP to an invitation, which means the host needs to know *whether or not you* will be attending. This is particularly important when you're invited to a large corporate or social event that requires a response.

> **When you accept an invitation, your response conveys a commitment that costs someone money.**

Here's the bottom line: When you accept an invitation, your response conveys a commitment that costs someone money. Not only that, the host, restaurant, caterer, or banquet planner needs to know how many tables to set up and meals to prepare.

Instead of "RSVP," some invitations say "Regrets Only." This means the host will presume you are able to attend unless you specifically decline the invitation.

No matter which of the two terms appears on the invitation, *if you can't go, say no!* It is disrespectful and unprofessional to commit to attending an event and then not show up.

If you've accepted an invitation and your plans change, let the host or event planner know *as soon as possible.* Your change of plans may open up an opportunity for someone on a waiting list or a secondary guest list to attend.

Sometimes, people are noticed for their absence as much as for their presence. At an executive seminar I once presented at an accounting firm, the managing partner spontaneously decided to make a public announcement to the group that one of their colleagues had just been made partner. The problem was, even though he had RSVP'd, when he was invited to the podium the newly promoted colleague was nowhere to be seen. Oops.

Dressing for the occasion

If you have even the slightest doubt about what to wear, contact your host, the venue, or the event planner and find out what's expected. You don't want to be the one in jeans and a t-shirt when everyone else is wearing business suits and ball gowns. Trust me on this one.

Themed events can be a challenge to dress for. Some people love wearing costumes, and others dread getting dressed up in medieval, retro, or masquerade garb. If you agree to attend a theme-based event, show some enthusiasm by creating or renting an appropriate outfit, and put some effort into playing your part. Otherwise, decline the invitation.

Common categories of dress indicators such as

"business casual" are vague and open to interpretation. While one man may construe that phrase to mean dress pants and a golf shirt, another may think it means wearing a blazer, tailored pants, and collared shirt, only omitting the tie. If you don't know what to wear, ask.

> *You don't need to host a summit to decide what to wear to an event. Find your inner fashionista and go for it!*

Women run into this conundrum all the time, commonly having a conversation like, "What are you wearing tonight?" followed by, "I don't know; what are you going to wear?" Seriously, you don't need to host a summit to decide what to wear to an event. Find your inner fashionista and go for it! To be safe, though, I recommend that when you're deciding between two outfits, choose the dressier one. It's preferable to be slightly overdressed than noticeably underdressed.

When it comes to formal meetings and job interviews, whether you're a man or a woman, I suggest you come prepared by at least *carrying* a blazer or jacket. What the heck, why not just wear it? You can always take it off—a much better option than wishing you had one to put on.

WTF? IS IT OKAY FOR A MAN TO TAKE OFF HIS SUIT JACKET OR BLAZER DURING A MEAL?

I advise leaving your tie and jacket or blazer on, and almost every gentleman I've questioned about this agrees. If the host, groom, or male guest of honor removes his jacket or invites others to remove theirs, then that's okay. The more formal the event, the more likely all of the men will wear their jackets throughout. If you're sweltering, others will be as well. You may be seen as a hero if you initiate the conversation that leads to agreeing to peel the outer layer. But remember, it's the host who ultimately sets the tone. By the way, if you want to remove your jacket when you're on a date or at a one-on-one meeting, say something like, "I'm finding it warm in here. Do you mind if I take off my jacket?"

Being punctual

Being on time is a show of respect for the host and other guests. Whether you're attending a casual dinner at someone's home or an elaborate event in a ballroom, late arrivals upset the flow of any event. The timing of a meal depends on the presence of the guests, making it inappropriate to be tardy. If you're going to be delayed, let the host or venue personnel know so schedules can be adjusted accordingly. If you do arrive late, don't make a big deal of it. Slip in quietly, take your seat, and join the conversation without sharing your drama.

Bringing gifts

When you're invited to someone's home, it's nice to bring

a small gift for the host or hostess. It doesn't need to be expensive; it simply needs to be thoughtful. If you bring a bottle of wine, don't expect your host to serve it on that occasion; he or she may have already planned the perfect pairing for the meal. Flowers are another great option; just be sure they're already in a vase so your host doesn't have to cut and arrange them on the spot. Other gift ideas include potted plants, interesting books or journals, chocolate, and seasonal ornaments. The more you know about the host, the more personalized you can make the gift.

Where to sit
At restaurants and in meeting rooms, wait for the host, maître d', or wait staff to show you to your seat. In someone's home, ask the host or hostess where they'd like you to sit if they don't lead you to a particular chair.

At large venues, there may be a seating plan at the front of the ballroom or a table number on your ticket. In these cases, you may seat yourself at your allotted place. It's never appropriate to rearrange place cards on a table; no doubt your host put a lot of thought into where guests will be seated.

If you bring a date or guest (sometimes referred to as a "plus-one") to an event, it is considerate to seat that person in the preferred position at the table to better enjoy the view or focus on the speaker or entertainment.

WTF? IS IT NECESSARY FOR MEN TO STAND WHEN A WOMAN LEAVES THE TABLE OR ENTERS THE ROOM?

In our gender-neutral business world, men are no longer expected to stand when a female colleague enters or exits the room. Nor do they need to pull out a woman's chair and assist her into her seat (but they still can if they want to). In social settings, however, doing so is a lovely gesture, and not just for your escort. It is thoughtful for a gentleman to rise and help a lady (or another man, for that matter), whether she's his daughter, his spouse, his date, or his mother-in-law. I know, I know—many people find this insulting and unnecessary. I urge you to consider the underlying kindness behind this action.

By the way, this deed isn't reserved just for men; there's no reason a female can't offer to help someone to a chair, too.

Where, when, and whether to order alcohol

At a business meal, it can be unnerving to decide if you should order an alcoholic beverage. There are no absolutes. Some businesses have corporate guidelines that prohibit consumption of alcohol on company time, while others have no problem with it whatsoever. I encourage you to develop and follow your own guiding principles, and always BYOB (Bring Your Own Behavior).

If you're looking for a job or an internship, keep in mind that some employers take prospective employees out for a meal in part to see how they respond when alcohol is offered. Unfortunately, you're not a mind reader.

Maybe they expect you to say yes to their offer because it shows you'll fit in with their corporate culture, or perhaps they expect you to say no because it goes against company policy.

> *Remember the words of legendary football coach Knute Rockne: "Drink the first. Sip the second slowly. Skip the third."*

Social circumstances usually present fewer issues about the appropriateness of having a drink during a meal. Remember, a good host will always invite you to order first, so waiting to see whether the host orders a drink before deciding if you will, doesn't work.

If you choose to order alcohol with your meal, whether at a business or a social event, I urge you to remember the words of legendary football coach Knute Rockne: "Drink the first. Sip the second slowly. Skip the third." And always pre-arrange a safe mode of transportation to get you back to your home or hotel safely if you've been drinking.

What matters most is that you always feel comfortable declining alcohol—whenever you wish and for whatever reason you want—without feeling a need to explain yourself to anyone. Ever. Period.

Selecting Wine

If, as a guest, you're asked to select the wine at a meal, only do so if you feel very comfortable with your level of wine knowledge so you know if your choice will pair well with the menu. Otherwise, decline or ask the waiter, host, or sommelier to make a recommendation based on their expertise. If you agree to order the wine, select a mid-priced bottle. After all, you'll be spending someone else's money.

Making toasts

At intimate gatherings, the host will likely make the initial toast once everyone is settled and drinks have been served. Sometimes, though, one of the guests may be the first to offer a toast.

Should you want to make a spontaneous toast to, for example, thank your host or salute someone's good news, stand and ask others to join you in celebrating. You don't need to clink glasses, but if everyone else does, be a good sport and go along with it.

If someone offers a toast to you, do not raise or clink your glass. Simply stay seated, look at people directly, smile, and say thank you afterwards. Sometimes you will be asked to respond to a toast, so it's a good idea to have a few points in mind to share.

At a wedding or similar formal event, there will usually be toasts of celebration or gratitude on the agenda.

If you've been asked to present a toast, come prepared and know at what point in the meal your host would like you to speak. Keep your tribute brief and to the point, and always stand when you speak.

Ordering your meal

Although your host may offer meal suggestions from the menu, he or she will normally invite you to order first. Avoid choosing finger foods or dishes that can be challenging to eat, like spaghetti, hamburgers, crab legs, big sandwiches, wraps, and ribs. If you order fries or pizza, use a knife and fork to eat them. Yes, really.

Handling special dietary requirements

If you've been invited to someone's home and you have food allergies or specific dietary needs, let your host know about your requirements when you accept the invitation. People need time to prepare exclusive meals and will appreciate advance notice.

If you'll be attending a large event, notify the caterer, event planner, or chef beforehand and say, in no uncertain terms, what your unique dietary needs are. Then, when you arrive at the event, diplomatically inform your server or the banquet captain that you ordered a special meal.

I've been at numerous dinners—both in restaurants and at people's homes—when the food was served and *then* someone said, "Oh, I'm on a gluten- (fat-, salt-, sugar-, wheat-, meat-, egg-, fish-, whatever-) free diet. Do you have something else I can eat?" Or, "Do you know if there's fill in the blank in this dish? I can't eat fill in the blank." By that time, it's often too late for the host or chef to create a special meal for you, and they might not even have the appropriate ingredients on hand. Take responsibility to communicate your needs well ahead of time.

Knowing when to start eating

At a sit-down meal, wait until everyone at your table has been served before you begin eating your food. If there's a host or a guest of honor, wait until that person either starts eating or says, "Please go ahead" before you dig in.

If you're dining at a buffet, it's good to talk with your tablemates *before* going to get your food to determine if the group prefers to wait until everyone returns to begin eating or will start as soon as each person is reseated. You could say something like, "Since we'll all be coming back to the table at different times, why don't we agree that we'll start eating as soon as we sit down rather than waiting for everyone to get back? That way we can all enjoy our food while it's hot. Sound like a plan?"

Sometimes it's necessary to send your food back to the kitchen because it's been prepared improperly. In that case, don't expect others to wait for you. Instead, invite them to go ahead and begin eating.

Understanding who should pay

Unless otherwise stated, *the person who invites you to join them for a meal normally pays the bill.* This isn't always the case, though; someone may simply ask to get together with you (or a group) and expect that you'll pay your own way.

Many people are unaware that one of their duties as a host is to pay the bill, so never presume that the cost of your meal will be taken care of. Always be prepared to pay for your own food. It's perfectly acceptable to inquire if you'll be responsible for your own meal by asking, "Shall we arrange for separate bills?"

When it comes to business, the company you work for may prohibit employees from accepting gifts, including gratuitous meals. It's good to check the corporate policy or ask someone in the know about specific restrictions.

Weddings and other social occasions are normally paid for in their entirety by the host, though a cash bar (requiring you to pay for your own drinks) may be in place. One exception to this is a destination wedding. In this case, invited guests are usually responsible for paying for their own travel and accommodations. Most often, the cost of the wedding meal is taken care of.

Visiting private clubs

If you're invited to a private club, be aware of the club's policies including parking, dress codes, and the use of cell phones and other electronic devices. Even if you disagree with the policies, you must observe them. Not doing so reflects negatively on the member who invited you and puts you in a bad light.

I was at a private club that had a clearly stated dress requirement for men to wear a jacket and tie. In the cloakroom was an interesting assortment of blazers and ties that had been donated by members for gentlemen who arrived unprepared. Trust me, you wouldn't want to be wearing one of those wardrobe loaners. Talk about a fashion statement!

When dining at a private club, also keep in mind that the bill will probably not come to the table, as members are usually invoiced monthly.

Expressing gratitude

It's imperative to say thank you to the person or people who invited you to join them for a meal. I recommend saying thank you twice; once verbally, either after the meal or when you're leaving the venue, and again the next day. Do it in writing. For some, that means sending an e-mail or text message. Yes, that will do. However, I strongly recommend you send a thoughtful, handwritten card by post.

PART FOUR

NAPKINS AND PLACE SETTINGS

" **... And the Dish ran away with the Spoon.**

Mother Goose "

OU'RE NOT ALONE if you've found yourself questioning what to do with your napkin or wondering whether you should sweep the breadcrumbs off the table. And the last thing you want to worry about when you sit down to enjoy a formal meal is which fork, bread plate, or dining style to use. Knowing about these details in advance will empower you to dine with dignity rather than fumble with faux pas.

NAPKINS

Using a napkin

From a strip of paper towel to hand-embroidered, mono-grammed linen, napkins (also called serviettes) come in a variety of sizes and materials. In addition, you'll find them placed in different locations on the table depending on the venue. One day, you may find your napkin on the left side of the place setting under the forks; another day, it may be folded like a swan and tucked in a wine glass or water goblet. Either way, once you sit down, where you place the napkin and how you use it should be consistent.

Placing your napkin

If you're hosting a meal, it's up to you to remove your napkin from the table *first*, once everyone is seated. Why? This signals your guests that the meal is about to begin. As a guest, watch for this cue from the host. Only then do you remove your napkin from the table.

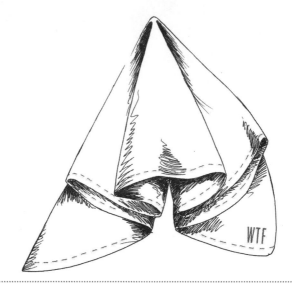

Napkins are meant for dabbing your lips, not blowing your nose or wiping your brow.

If there is no host or your host is unfamiliar with napkin use, wait for everyone to take a seat, then remove your napkin from the table. And whatever you do, don't vigorously unfurl, shake, or snap your napkin! Always place it on your lap, never in your shirt collar or between your buttons. It can be hard to have a serious conversation with someone who's outfitted like a toddler with a bib on!

When you put the napkin on your lap, keep it folded in half and place the crease toward your waist. In certain restaurants, the waiter will place your napkin on your lap for you. Don't freak out if this happens; just go with it! If you're wearing a dark color, the wait staff may exchange your white napkin with a black one to avoid transferring lint to your clothing.

If you need to dab your lips during the meal, leave the bottom half of the napkin on your lap and just bring the top part to your mouth. That way you can place the soiled napkin fabric back on top of the clean half that remains on your lap and avoid dirtying your clothing.

Leaving the table during a meal

First of all, if you need to leave the table, there is no need to announce where you're going. A simple "excuse me, please" will do. And by the way, ladies, there's no need to invite a posse of your pals to escort you to the restroom. Just sayin'.

There are different schools of thought about where to place the napkin if you leave the table during the meal. My advice is to place your napkin on the seat of your chair. This is based on two things: (1) people's disinterest in seeing your soiled serviette on the table in their line of vision while they're eating, and (2) history—long before washing machines existed it was easier to launder a napkin than a tablecloth. People would therefore keep their napkin off the tablecloth to minimized the risk of soiling it.

Others, however, disagree with my perspective, saying they find the mere thought of putting their napkin on the seat of the chair disgusting. Then some diners declare they're concerned about dirtying the chair seat—and subsequently their backside—when they are re-seated. This camp opts to put the napkin on the arm of the chair or the left side of the place setting during an absence.

I still recommend placing it on your chair seat. No matter what you choose to do, when you return from your jaunt, discreetly replace the napkin on your lap.

> *You do not need to refold your napkin at the end of your meal. In fact, you might find refolding it impossible—especially if it started out looking like a swan!*

Ending the meal

After eating, the host indicates the meal is ending by placing his or her napkin on the table (not on the plate!). You may then place your napkin on the table, too, to the left of your plate. If there is no host, wait until it looks like people have finished eating their meals before placing your napkin on the table. You do *not* need to refold it. In fact, you might find refolding it impossible—especially if it started out looking like a swan!

WTF? WHAT ARE SOME NAPKIN NO-NO'S?

Napkins are meant to be used for dabbing your lips and blotting unexpected drips while dining. They also come in handy to dry your fingers if your glass has condensation on it or if you're served food that requires the use of your hands. Napkins are not meant to double as aprons, brow-wipes, or facial tissue. Refrain from blowing your nose into a napkin, especially a cloth napkin. Not only is it gross, it's even more off-putting when you consider another person will be using that napkin shortly after you do. Yes, it will be laundered between uses, but still . . .

PLACE SETTINGS

You can generally tell what courses will be served by looking at your place setting. Forks are normally to the left of the plate and knives and spoons are on the right. However, if you see a small fork on the right side of your plate (sometimes resting partially in the spoon), it likely means you will be served something like a shrimp cocktail as an appetizer or first course.

The placement of your silverware is like a chart to help you understand which piece of flatware to choose for each course. When selecting a utensil, start from the outside of the place setting and work toward the plate as each course is served.

Servers typically remove used silverware when clearing each course. In formal settings, expect to see both a fork and a knife for your salad as well as for your entrée. Once you have removed a piece of silverware from the table, even the handle shouldn't touch the table again; it rests on your plate.

The butter knife rests on the bread plate, which is normally placed above or beside the forks on the left. A dessertspoon and fork are commonly paired and placed above your plate. A variety of glassware, including water goblets, champagne flutes, and wine glasses, are placed on the right, above the utensils. Your coffee or tea cup and saucer, which will usually be provided after the meal, are placed on the right side as well.

WTF

PART FIVE

DINING STYLES
AND SILVERWARE

"

The way you cut your meat reflects the way you live.

Confucius

"

ANY VARIATIONS of dining styles exist, sometimes even among members of the same family! Here, let's look at the two most common styles of formal dining, *Continental* and *North American*. As the names suggest, the latter style is unique to North America, while the Continental style is more commonly practiced in other locations around the globe.

Both styles start and finish the same, with the fork in the left hand and the knife in the right. The biggest difference is that in the *Continental* style, the fork stays in the left hand for eating after the food is cut, while in the *North American* style, the fork is moved to the right hand for eating (lefties, see WTF? box on page 93).

Another difference is that in the *Continental* style, the fork tines (the pointy ends) are always facing *down*, while in the *North American* style they are rotated to the *up* position when the fork is transferred to the right hand.

Each style has a "rest" and a "finished" position for the placement of the silverware. Positioning yours in the appropriate place silently signals your server that you are either taking a break or finished your meal.

CONTINENTAL STYLE

The fork is in the left hand and knife is in the right hand for cutting food (remember, for some left-handed people the opposite feels more natural). Your silverware remains in these hands throughout the meal. In the *Continental* style, fork tines are always *down* while dining (even when you're eating rice or peas!) and when resting on the plate.

In the *Continental* style, you indicate you are resting by placing your knife and fork on the plate in an upside-down V position, like this Λ. Another way to remember the Continental rest position is to imagine your plate is a clock. Place your knife handle at about the 5 and your fork handle at about the 7. Fork tines are down, and the knife blade faces toward the center of the plate, not the outer rim. Remember, the handles of your silverware do not touch the table; rather, they rest on the plate (see fig.1).

The finished position for the *Continental* style is when both pieces of silverware are placed side by side on the right side of the plate, angled at about the 5 position. The fork is to the left of the knife and the knife blade is facing the fork, tines up. *This is the only time in Continental dining that fork tines are up* (see fig.2).

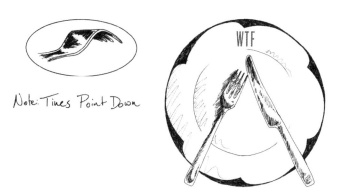

Note: Tines Point Down

fig.1 Continental Rest Position

In the Continental style of dining, this position indicates to your server that you are taking a momentary break from eating. **Note that the fork tines are down.**

Note: fork tines facing up

fig.2 Continental Finished Position

Place your knife and fork in this position when you have finished your meal. This is the **only** time in the Continental style when the tines are up.

The *Continental* style may feel awkward at first, like your fork is upside-down. Try piercing a piece of firm food with your fork. Then use your knife to position less stable food on the flat part of the fork.

NORTH AMERICAN STYLE

For cutting food in the *North American* style, the fork is in the left hand and the knife is in the right hand (again, the opposite may feel more comfortable for left-handed people). Remember not to cut all your food at once; slice only one or two small bites at a time.

After cutting, the knife is then rested on the right side of the plate with the blade facing the center, not the outer rim. No part of the knife should be in contact with the table. The fork is now switched to the right hand for eating, and the tines are up.

Rest position for the *North American* style is with the knife and fork on the right side of the plate, slightly apart and a bit higher on the plate than for the finished position. The knife is to the right of the fork, the fork tines are up, and the serrated edge of the knife is facing toward the fork. The flatware never touches the table (see fig.3).

The *North American* finished position is the same as in the *Continental* style, with both pieces of silverware together at about the 5 position. The fork tines are up and the fork is to the left of the knife. The knife blade is facing the fork (see fig.4).

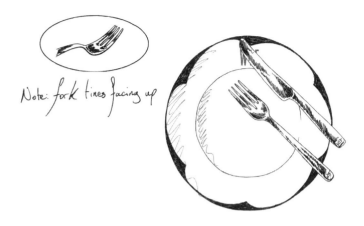

Note: fork tines facing up

fig.3 North American Rest Position

In the North American style, place your silverware like this to indicate you are pausing to rest. **The fork tines are up.**

Note: fork tines facing up

fig.4 North American Finished Position

This is the finished position for the North American styles of dining. It is the same as the Continental style—this is the **only** time in the Continental style when the tines are up.

HOLDING SILVERWARE

As noted, this book outlines the two most common styles of dining, *North American* and *Continental*. No matter which style you practice, you begin by holding the fork in your left hand and the knife in your right hand. Make sure to place the handles of the silverware in your palms instead of clutching them with a closed fist or wedging them between your fingers (lefties, see WTF? box on page 93).

By the way, if you ever drop a piece of silverware on the floor in a restaurant, signal a waiter or bus person and ask for it to be replaced. Only move it yourself if it is a hazard. If you drop a dining utensil at someone's home, it's fine to pick it up and ask your host for another one.

fig.5 Holding your silverware properly

To make sure you are holding your flatware properly, try this exercise. Open your left hand with your palm facing up. Rest a dinner fork diagonally in the palm of your hand, with the end of the handle at the base of your palm below your baby finger, and the part where the tines (pointy parts of the fork) meet the handle resting near the tip of your index finger. The tines should be up and pointing at the ceiling.

fig.6 Holding your silverware properly

Now, keeping your index finger extended, close your other fingers and the thumb of that hand around the handle. Grasp it loosely, and turn your hand over so your palm and the tines are facing down.

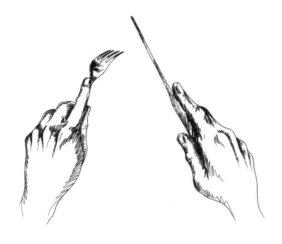

fig.7 Holding your silverware properly

Do the same with a dinner knife in your right hand, placing the juncture where the blade meets the handle near the tip of your index finger. The serrated knife edge points down. This is how you hold a fork and knife.

fig.8 The proper way to hold a soupspoon

A soupspoon is held similarly to how you hold a pencil.

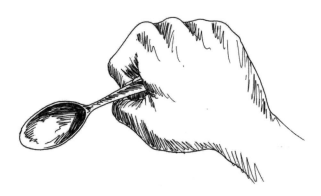

fig.9 How NOT to hold a soupspoon

Don't clutch it in a fisted hand like a toothbrush.

WTF? WHAT IF I'M LEFT-HANDED?

Many left-handed people are comfortable holding the knife in their right hand and the fork in their left. And, while this is correct, some left-handed people tell me it feels awkward, so they reverse which piece of silverware they hold in each hand, as well as the placement of the flatware on the plate when in the resting position.

If you intend to follow stringent dining protocols (whether you are right- or left-handed), I recommend learning how to to manoeuvre silverware with the fork in your left hand and the knife in your right. That said, the rules of formal dining have loosened, and yours is a personal preference. Either way, the formal place setting and the finished position remain the same for left- and right-handed diners. For the purposes of this book, examples for right-hand dominant people have been provided.

PART SIX

COURSES

"

Dinner is not what you do in the evening before something else. Dinner is the evening.

Art Buchwald

"

HE NUMBER OF COURSES served at a formal meal will vary from event to event. In someone's home, for example, you may be offered a simple, though very formal, 3-course lunch or dinner of salad, entrée, and dessert. But you could also find yourself at a Michelin-starred restaurant or sitting at a Chef's Table where 15 courses (or more!) are served, each one with much pomp and ceremony. Remember, the place-setting in front of you is your biggest clue about how many courses to expect. As well, there is often a formally printed menu card on the table, which outlines the details of the meal. Here's what you can expect at a basic formal dinner, starting with cocktails and ending with dessert.

BEVERAGES

When circulating the room—say at a pre-dinner reception—hold your beverage in your left hand (if permitted in your culture) to free up your right hand for shaking hands and presenting your business or calling card.

Hold a long-stemmed glass—like a champagne flute or wine glass—by the stem. If you order a beer or a soda that comes in a bottle or can, it will usually be presented either in a glass or with a glass on the side. If the server doesn't pour the beverage into the glass for you, do so yourself.

When using a cup and saucer for tea or coffee, the saucer stays on the table and the cup is lifted to your mouth. If drinking coffee or tea while standing, hold the saucer in one hand while bringing the cup to your mouth with the other.

Stir beverages quietly; there's no need to create a vortex! Avoid clinking your spoon against the side of the cup or glass. Never put a wet, sticky spoon on the table linen; place it on the saucer after stirring.

APPETIZERS

Appetizers may be served to whet your appetite at a pre-meal reception or to start a meal. If offered at a reception, they're often small portions of food that are artfully presented and meant to be eaten with your fingers or from a skewer or cocktail stick.

To keep your right hand clean and available for shaking hands at a reception, I suggest eating any kind of "finger food" with your left hand unless this is disallowed in your culture.

PART EIGHT

GRATITUDE AND FOLLOW UP

When appetizers are served as part of a meal, you will normally have the necessary silverware delivered or already at your place setting. If an accompanying dip or sauce is served with an appetizer, place some on your plate rather than dipping your food in the serving bowl.

WTF? WHAT IS AN AMUSE-BOUCHE?

An amuse-bouche is a small, beautifully prepared morsel of food that is often offered to diners before a meal as a surprise gift from the chef. Loosely translated, amuse-bouche means "amuse the mouth." This special hors d'oeuvre is usually either a house specialty or a delicacy that has been created by the chef to complement the menu. It's meant to tickle your taste buds and prepare you for what lies ahead.

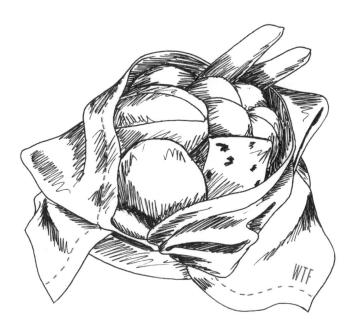

BREAD

"Which bread plate is mine?" is one of the most common questions people ask at a formal dining table. Sometimes it's hard to tell, when there are so many pieces of china, crystal, and flatware on the table.

Your bread plate is the small one on the left side of the place setting, usually above the forks (remember, in BMW, B = Bread). It has a butter knife or spreader placed diagonally on it. Imagine your plate is a clock; the handle will be pointing at the 4 (see fig.10).

Bread—in the shape of rolls, sticks, or a loaf—can be served in a breadbasket, already on your bread plate, or

offered by the waiter who puts it on your bread plate using tongs.

When buns or bread are served in a basket, you almost always find the inside of the basket lined with a cloth, which also covers the bread. This cloth serves two purposes: (1) to keep bread fresh or warm, and (2) to allow you to select the piece you want without touching the others that you don't want. To do this, place your hand on the fabric and use the fabric to move the rolls or bread you don't want to get to the one you do. This principle also applies to loaves of bread served whole on a breadboard with a cutting knife. You can use the cloth to hold the bread steady while slicing it for the group, hence never touching the bread itself.

When there is a breadbasket on the table—and once everyone has been seated and settled—the host (if there is one) can initiate the dining process by asking if anyone would like bread. Then the host, or whoever is closest to the breadbasket, takes it off the table, and can then do one of two things, either (a) while holding the basket, offer bread to the person on the left, or (b) pass the entire breadbasket to the person on the right. This is where things can get confusing!

In scenario (a), if you're the one to the left of the person offering the bread, you are meant to take just a piece of bread, not the whole basket. Because food is passed to the right, the kind person next to you is simply offering

you some bread so you don't have to wait for the basket to make its way around the table. After that little exchange, whether you accept or decline the offer of bread, the person holding the basket may take a piece for him or herself before passing the basket to the person on the right.

In scenario (b), which is equally acceptable, the person who takes the breadbasket from the table offers the whole basket to the person on the right without considering the person on the left or taking a piece of bread for him or herself first. If you are the person on the right of the breadbasket offerer, you now have a decision to make. You can either accept the breadbasket, take your piece of bread, and pass the basket along to the person on *your* right OR say to the person who offered it to you, "After you." Who knew passing bread could be so complicated? And this is just the beginning of the meal!

Passing the butter follows passing the bread. If you don't want any, accept the butter dish and offer it to the person on your right. If you choose to use butter, take an appropriate amount from the butter dish and place it on the side of your bread plate. Please don't slap a mountain of butter on your plate; you can always ask for more after others have taken what they need.

If foil-wrapped butter pats are served (which would not happen at a really formal meal), remove the wrapping and put the butter on your bread plate using your butter knife. The folded foil can be folded and placed there as well.

Sometimes the butter dish will have its own small fork or dedicated butter knife for you to use to take a pat or portion of butter. In this case, put the butter on your bread plate and replace the common butter fork or knife on the butter plate before passing it to the person on your right.

fig.10 Which bread plate is mine?

Your bread plate is the small one on the left side of the place setting, usually above the forks. Note the position of the knife on the plate.

If someone mistakenly uses your bread plate (a common occurrence), ask the server for another one. Or, if your entree has been served and someone else is using your bread plate, you may consider placing your

bread on your dinner plate. If the entire group is using the wrong bread plate, it's best to not make a scene. Just go with the flow.

Buns and bread are meant to be broken into small pieces with your fingers, not cut with a knife. Holding the bread or bun over your bread plate, break it ONE bite-sized piece at a time, butter that small piece, and eat it. Do not saw your bun like a steak or ice your bread with butter like it's a cake.

If you're at a formal brunch and served toast, it is acceptable to cut each piece in half or quarters and add butter or other spreads. Just remember not to put your "crumby" knife in the common butter or spread; instead, use the knife or spoon provided for that purpose.

WTF? WHAT ABOUT ALL THOSE CRUMBS?

Crumbs will naturally fall to the table when you eat bread, especially the crusty, grainy, or seedy kind. Your waiter may come along with a crumb knife or roller to clean them up. If that doesn't happen, leave the remnants where they land. You don't need to feel obligated to sweep them off the table.

Your soup may be served in a cup, a bowl, or a soup plate (which is shallow and looks similar to a pasta bowl). The cup, bowl, or soup plate usually rests on what is called an "under plate."

Once everyone has been served, and following your host's lead, remove the soupspoon from the right side of your place setting and put it in your soup at about the middle of the bowl. Moving the spoon *away* from you, fill it about two-thirds of the way with soup. Gather any drips on the back rim of the bowl and, maintaining erect posture, bring the soup to your mouth (not your mouth to the soup).

Believe it or not, there is a difference in how you eat clear soup versus creamy or chunky soup. There are even different soupspoons for use with each type. A clear soup-spoon—used for broth and consommé—is more oval, long, and slender than a cream soupspoon, which is rounder and deeper.

> **Believe it or not, there is a difference in how you eat clear soup versus creamy or chunky soup.**

To eat clear soup, bring the spoon to your mouth and, placing it sideways on your lower lip, tip the soup into your mouth rather than putting the whole spoon in your mouth. For creamy or chunky soups, the entire spoon goes into your mouth. Either way, you don't want to slurp!

Rest your spoon on the under plate between bites and when you are finished. This isn't always possible, however. Sometimes, like when a soup plate is used, there isn't room to place your spoon on the under plate. In that case, rest it in the soup plate.

To get the last spoonful of soup, be sure to tip the bowl *away* from you. Expect the server to remove your soup-spoon when taking your bowl away.

In the Introduction to *What The Fork?*, I said even let-tuce deserves to be treated with respect. Here's why: many "soft" lettuces and greens, such as butter lettuce and arugula, are considered delicate and can easily bruise. Because of this, it's best to fold, not cut, them using a salad fork and knife together. However, hard lettuce that has a core, like romaine, needs to be cut.

It can be challenging to fold lettuce at first, but I assure you that with practice, it becomes easy. Using the salad fork and salad knife—which are smaller versions of the entrée fork and knife, and should be at the outside of your place setting—pierce a piece or two of lettuce with your fork and use your knife to fold the lettuce, re-piercing it with your fork as you make a little bundle. Other vegeta-bles in the salad—like tomato, carrot, or cucumber—can be cut and pierced with the fork to "anchor" the lettuce on the tines.

Once you feel confident that the bundle is secure on your fork, bring it to your mouth. If you choose the *Continental* style of dining, the fork will remain in your left hand with the tines down. You'd transfer it to your right hand for the *North American* style, resting your knife on the side of your plate or salad bowl.

If dressing is served separately, pour or spoon an adequate amount on your salad, and then pass the dressing to the person on your right. As an aside, sometimes dressing (or gravy) is served in a "boat" ~ it's like a little pitcher with a handle, and it is usually resting on a plate. If there is no spoon or ladle on the plate, pour the dressing or gravy directly on your food. If there is a spoon or ladle, however, use it to transfer the liquid to your food.

It is important to note that sometimes (though rarely) at a formal dinner the salad is served after the entrée and before dessert. Your place setting is your best guide to ascertain which order the meal will be served in, so take note.

SORBET

Often, in preparation for the upcoming entrée, a small amount of sorbet is served to cleanse your palate after the salad course. This refreshing iced treat comes in a variety of flavors (usually fruity) and is eaten with a spoon, which will either have been pre-set on the right side of your place setting or be served with the sorbet.

Always test the firmness of the sorbet before you dig in; if it's really frozen, it could fly out of the bowl like a hockey puck!

ENTRÉE

After the salad and associated flatware have been removed, you'll be left with a large knife and a large fork at your place setting. These are used to eat your entrée, the main course. Hold each utensil as described earlier and pierce the meat or vegetable with the fork, cutting it with the knife one piece at a time.

Remember, for the *Continental* style, your fork remains in your left hand with the tines down for eating. In the *North American* style, you rest your knife on the right side of the plate after cutting and then switch the fork to your right hand with the tines up to eat.

Avoid using a piece of bread or your thumb to place the food on your fork; instead, use your knife in unison with the fork to manipulate the placement of the food. Never lick your knife or talk with food in your mouth, and avoid waving your silverware around like you're conducting an orchestra.

At a formal meal, dessert often includes a solid and a liquid—such as pie and ice cream—so it typically requires both a spoon and fork to eat. The flavors are meant to be savored together, which is why both pieces of silverware are used together.

Sometimes dessert silverware will be brought to you when dessert is served, but usually the dessertspoon and fork are pre-positioned at the top of your place setting, with the spoon above the fork (as illustrated on the pull out insert). You will note that normally the fork handle faces left and the spoon handle faces right.

If the dessertspoon and fork are at the top of your place setting, move them to either side of your dessert plate once dessert has been served (or your waiter may do this for you). The fork is placed on the left side of the plate and the spoon on the right side.

With the spoon in your right hand and the fork simultaneously in your left hand, use the fork to lightly pierce the "solid" part of the dessert. Hold it steady as you coax (not saw) a piece of the solid apart *with your spoon*. Gently place the food on the spoon with your fork and scoop some of the liquid with your spoon. Then enjoy the mingled flavors (see fig. 11, 12 and 13).

If your dessert is soft and smooth—like crème brûlée or pudding—and has no "solid" component, use only your dessertspoon. If it is something like cake or tiramisu—and has no "liquid" element—use only the fork. In these situations, you would leave the other utensil on the table.

Berries are typically eaten with a spoon, but if a whole strawberry is served, for example, you may need to use both pieces of silverware as described above to cut it into bite-sized pieces.

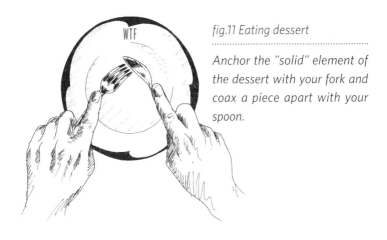

fig.11 Eating dessert

Anchor the "solid" element of the dessert with your fork and coax a piece apart with your spoon.

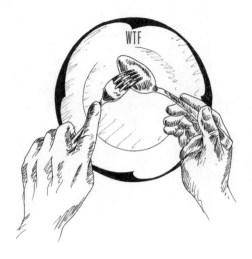

fig.12 Eating dessert

Use your fork to place the solid piece of dessert onto your spoon.

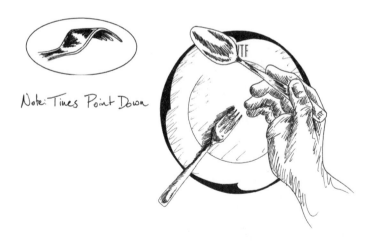

Note: Tines Point Down

fig.13 Eating dessert

Scoop some of the "liquid" (like ice cream or coulis) with your spoon to blend with the "solid" element. Leave the fork on the plate, tines down, and eat from your spoon.

PART SEVEN

ADDITIONAL
DETAILS

"

Dining is and always was a great artistic opportunity.

Frank Lloyd Wright

"

*T*HERE IS MUCH MORE to a meal than just the food. You need to know how to carry on a conversation, what to do if you find yourself in an awkward situation, and even where to put your smartphone or purse! It's details like these that elevate simple eating to the level of formal dining.

HOW TO BEHAVE AT THE TABLE

Anticipating the service
Guests are usually served before the host (head table notwithstanding), and at most formal meals, women will be served before men.

The direction of service and removal of plates varies from venue to venue. While most waiters serve from the left and remove from the right, others serve and remove from the same side. This depends on a variety of elements, including the layout of the room and how the staff was trained.

Pay attention to whether the server approaches from your left or right side. That way, you can move slightly if necessary to accommodate service as your meal arrives.

Unless you're in a booth or at a banquette table (a table that is attached to the wall), your drinks will normally be served from the right. This is because that's where your drinking glasses are (W = anything Wet!). It can be risky for servers to pour across a person's body, especially when the beverage is hot.

Clearing the table

There is no need for you to scrape and stack the plates when you've finished eating. Just place your silverware in the finished position, leave your napkin on your lap, and let the waiter or busser clear the table. The server or bus person will usually wait until everyone at the table has finished eating before gathering the used tableware.

Passing and seasoning food

Food is normally passed to the right, but if your host or everyone else at the table starts passing to the left, go with the flow. Salt and pepper are passed together, even if only one is requested. That's because even though one person may only want to use salt, the person seated next to him or her may want both salt and pepper.

It's best to taste your food before adding spices or condiments, especially in someone's home, because you want to demonstrate respect for the chef's or cook's seasoning acumen.

Sharing food

It's almost a given that at some point in time someone at your table will offer or ask to share a bite of food. The more formal the circumstance, the less appropriate it is to share food. It's best to just say, "No, thanks."

> *Don't take their fork out of their hand, have them feed you like a child, or use your own fork to steal from their plate.*

If you're in an *informal* environment and one of your dining companions insist on sharing ("*Mmmmmm, you just haaaave to try this!*") what do you do? First of all, you can always decline. But if you simply can't resist, make sure they're close enough, both in distance and in friendship, to accept their offer. Then discreetly pass your bread plate to them to put a bite of food on. Don't take the fork out of their hand, have them feed you like a child, or use your own fork to steal from their plate. And don't even *think* about sharing food at a formal meal.

If you and your dinner date want to split one or two entrées in a restaurant, ask the server to have them plated half and half in the kitchen. Please note that many restaurants charge an additional fee to do this. Again, do *not* do

this at a formal meal; simply eat what you've been served in that environment.

Pacing yourself

Whether you eat quickly or slowly, keep an eye on the general pace of other diners at your table and adjust your speed accordingly. You don't want to be halfway through dessert when others are just starting their entrée.

WTF? IS THERE A SPECIFIC CALCULATION FOR CHEWING FOOD?

A surprising number of people ask me how many times they should chew their food before swallowing. There is no hard and fast number for this. Chew enough times so your food is ground to the point that it's not a choking hazard and is easy to swallow. If you are a fast eater and you need to slow down, extra chewing is one way to do so. It's preferable to take your time and savor the flavors than it is to feel like you have to count your crunches.

Grooming at the table

While out for dinner one evening, my husband and I watched in astonishment as the woman at the next table flossed her teeth—front to back, top to bottom—after eating her meal. Then the scene got worse. She handed her dining companion *the same strand of dental floss*, and he re-used it on his pearly whites. Needless to say, this public display of dental hygiene took a bite out of our appetites.

Activities like combing your hair, filing your fingernails, and picking your teeth should be performed in the privacy of the restroom. Period. This applies to both men and women. The jury is out on applying lipstick, lip-gloss, or lip balm at the table. I advise against doing this but must admit, I've done so myself. If you simply can't stand it and need to put something on your lips, do it inconspicuously and quickly.

The bottom line is this: don't get out a mirror and attend to your personal grooming in public. After all, you're in a dining room, not a powder room.

Wearing your hat

We wear hats for religious, cultural, medical, tribal, social, activity, climatic, and ceremonial reasons. Some service groups, for example, require members to wear a hat or headdress as part of their formal wear. I've attended many banquets where the gentlemen wear their uniform hat into the dining room, removing it only when the group's leader removes his as part of the established protocols of the organization.

Generally speaking, we've become very casual in Western society about when and we wear hats, which have made a huge comeback as a fashion accessory (I'm not referring to ball caps here, by the way!). And though the rules have relaxed in many informal dining situations, some things never change in formal circumstances. Ladies may wear an elegant hat that complements their outfit

during a social meal (just don't choose a big distracting one that will interfere with other people's view). The basic rule of thumb for you, gentlemen, is to remove your hat when you enter a dining room or someone's home, unless you are wearing it for a reason similar to those cited above. I'll even go as far as suggesting we all remove our hats, even for casual meals at home or in a restaurant!

Placing purses, briefcases, and electronic gadgetry
Have you ever been at a beautifully set table loaded with so much personal paraphernalia that eating the meal becomes a challenging obstacle course? The more formal the event, the less you want to mess with the beauty of the table setting. Therefore, ladies, if you're carrying a small clutch or handbag and your chair has a full back, simply place the purse at the small of your back between your body and the chair. I strongly advise against hanging a long-strapped purse or briefcase on the back of your chair. It can fall off and become a tripping hazard on the floor, or it can get stolen. If you have a backpack, tablet, briefcase, or large purse, it's best to place it on the floor near your feet.

It is almost impossible to get away from the omnipresent electronic devices in dining rooms around the globe. What a distraction! As a reaction, many restaurants have adopted "cell free" policies and request phone ringers be turned off out of respect for other diners. Here's an acronym I created to help you remember: TOYS. It stands for Turn Off Your Stuff. If you are expecting an urgent call or

text, let others at your table know in advance. And when it comes in, politely excuse yourself to take care of the call or text away from the table. Above all, be considerate.

When attending performances, formal, or ceremonial events, it's preferable to turn your smartphone off or leave it in the car or at home. If you do bring it with you, check, check, and check again that the ringer, buzzer, and all other sounds are SILENCED.

If you absolutely must take a call in the presence of other diners (which you would *not* do during a formal meal), be sure to turn off your speakerphone, keep your voice down, and use appropriate language. It really is best to leave the table and talk somewhere private.

Turning "nonversations" into conversations

Whether you're the host or the guest at a meal, you can turn "nonversations" into conversations by doing some research before arriving so you have something interesting to discuss. For example, if there's a guest speaker, find out about that person's background by doing an Internet search. Or, if you're attending a charity event, check out the organization's website and educate yourself on its purpose and key players. If an event is sponsored, learn about the sponsor's involvement and purpose ahead of time. That way, if you meet one of the benefactors or representatives, you can have a more meaningful—and memorable—discussion.

Most people like to talk about themselves, so ask them to share their stories. And then listen extremely carefully to what they have to say. Show your attentiveness by saying something like, "That sounds so interesting; please tell me more," or asking, "Can you please give me an example to help me understand better?"

> *Open-ended questions will almost always lead to more interesting conversations than questions that can be answered with yes or no.*

One of my favorite questions to ask someone who tends to constantly "talk shop" is, "What do you love to do when you're not working?" I usually learn so much more than when I inquire about where they work or whether they've been busy. Open-ended questions will almost always lead to more interesting conversations than questions that can be answered with yes or no.

For business meals, which are really just meetings disguised as eating, do your homework and come prepared to discuss the agenda. Avoid bringing reams of paper with you. Instead, either send the necessary documents prior to the meeting, or let your companion(s) know you'll forward the pertinent information to them afterwards.

Bringing food home

As much as you may want to, avoid the temptation to have your leftovers boxed up so you can take them home after a formal dinner. I was at an event where someone asked to have table scraps from all the diners packed up for their dog that "just loves steak!" Go to the butcher for Bowser; your host wants to feed *you*, not your pooch.

AWKWARD SITUATIONS

What happens if one of your dining companions gets food on their face or between their teeth? Or has something in their nostrils? Perhaps they suffer a wardrobe malfunction. What do you do? Breaking the news can be challenging, but it's important to let them know so they can correct the problem and save embarrassment.

As diplomatically and as privately as possible, lean in and quietly state a fact like, "Jody, you have a bit of lipstick on your teeth," or, "Barry, there's something on your cheek," or, "Jamie, your zipper has come undone." Less is more.

Heated exchanges

Conversations can go sideways during a meal, especially if someone passionately expresses an opinion about a contentious issue. I advise that if you can't change the tone, change the topic, and if you can't change the topic, change the location.

How do you change the location? Well, if you're at home when an awkward situation happens, try inviting everyone to a different room to divert the dialogue. You could say, "Let's move to the living room for dessert." Or you could interrupt the banter by asking for help, saying, "Barb, would you mind lending me a hand in the kitchen?" Most times, including in a restaurant, a simple change of topic can redirect an uncomfortable discussion. However, if things get out of hand, it's up to the host to deal with it. And if it's the host who gets out of hand, find a way to exit the situation altogether.

WTF? ARE THERE TOPICS THAT SHOULDN'T BE BROUGHT UP DURING A MEAL?

Just like your elbows, there are certain subjects that should stay off the table, and I came up with a way to help you remember what they are. No matter where the meal is taking place or what its purpose, remember the word DINE when determining whether or not something is appropriate to discuss. If a topic is Disgusting, Insulting, Nasty, or Embarrassing, keep it to yourself. The same applies to any subject that is overly emotional; there's a time and a place for those conversations to occur.

Physical catastrophes
Accidents can—and do—happen. I once bumped the elbow of a woman who was enjoying a glass of red wine while wearing an ivory-colored dress. You can imagine what followed! Thankfully, I had a silk wrap to offer her

so she could immediately cover the spill. Then I found out her name and contact information and, the next morning, couriered to her a personal note and gift certificate for dry cleaning. You convey a sincere apology with actions like this.

> *If you simply can't bear the thought of ingesting an item on your plate, don't eat it. However, depending on the situation, you may need to weigh the consequences of your decision.*

Unpalatable food
At some point, you will no doubt be served food that you don't like, don't want, or have never seen before. The smaller the group you're with, the more awkward this becomes. Sometimes you just have to suck it up and eat unfamiliar or unappetizing food.

If you simply can't bear the thought of ingesting an item on your plate, don't eat it. However, depending on the situation, you may need to weigh the consequences of your decision. In some circumstances, people may be deeply offended if you refuse to eat what they offer.

If the taste or texture of something you've put in your mouth turns your stomach, try to down it with a drink of water. Ultimately, you could discreetly remove it by cupping one hand over your mouth and quickly taking it out with the other hand or a utensil, placing it on the side of your plate. The same applies to things like gristle and bones.

Don't spit any kind of food onto your plate or into a cloth napkin unless it's some kind of dining emergency. My friend John was once caught by a surprise sneeze immediately after taking a mouthful of rice in a restaurant. He didn't quite get his napkin to his mouth in time and the rice flew on to the table, his dining companion—and even as far as the next table. Clearly he had no other choice but to use his napkin for damage control.

If something like that ever happens to you, signal the waiter and ask for a new napkin after you've calmed yourself down, cleaned yourself up, and made the necessary apologies.

Undercooked or incorrect food

If your meal is undercooked or otherwise incorrect, it's okay to ask for it to be heated or replaced. As noted earlier, don't expect others to wait for you while this happens; invite them to go ahead and eat while their food is fresh.

WTF? IS IT OKAY TO CORRECT PEOPLE WHO ARE NOT DINING PROPERLY?

The short answer is no. Look, there are as many ways to dine as there are ingredients in a chef's kitchen. Even etiquette books and advice columns vary in their recommendations. Most of us learned our table manners from caring people who did their very best to demonstrate what they believed was the most appropriate form. I'm not suggesting they were wrong; I'm simply offering a couple of other formal styles you may not have been aware of. No matter whose advice you follow and what style you adopt, knowing how to dine correctly doesn't give anyone the right to correct others. If someone asks for help or instruction, fine, but avoid pointing out the failings of your dining companions. Doing so is embarrassing, disrespectful, and unnecessary.

"

When we give cheerfully and accept gratefully, everyone is blessed.

Maya Angelou

"

*S*O MUCH WORK goes into making a meal a success, which is why you must go out of your way to say thank you after the event. If you organized and hosted the meal, remember to express your sincere gratitude to everyone who helped. And if you were lucky enough to be a guest, it's important to thank the host, your table mates, and the professionals who prepared and served the meal. You also want to follow up on any commitments you made during the meal, like calling or e-mailing people if you said you would be in touch.

SHARING APPRECIATION

Thank you notes
Sure, an e-mail or phone call expressing your gratitude will do, and depending on the nature of your relationship, that may be all you need. But though it may seem prehistoric to some, there's still something powerful to be said about sending handwritten notes. I hear from people all

the time who tell me how much they appreciate receiving a heartfelt thank you note. After all, if someone has been generous enough to invite you to a meal (and pay for it), you can be courteous enough to send a message of appreciation.

A simple thank you note

Three simple lines are all it takes to share your gratitude: *Thank you for _____. I especially enjoyed the _____. I look forward to seeing you again soon (or) good luck on your job hunt (or) I hope Carol and you have a wonderful vacation (or) I trust everything will work out.* Whatever you write, make it sincere and authentic. Take extra time to relate one of the points in your note to a conversation you had as a way to show you were listening.

For formal business correspondence, I recommend sending thank you notes via traditional post on corporate logo-embossed cardstock. Remember to include your business card if the recipient is a new contact.

For social notes, either have customized stationery printed, or purchase quality thank you notes. Avoid cutesy cards with puppies, rainbows, kittens, or unicorns on them (unless you're sending a thank you note to someone who is fascinated by puppies, rainbows, kittens, or unicorns!). Always send a note of gratitude when someone presents you with a gift.

WTF? DO I HAVE TO SAY THANK YOU TO THE SERVERS AND STAFF?

A meal cannot be a success without the employees of the restaurant or caterer. From servers and chefs to bus staff and front-of-the-house personnel, these people work hard and deserve to be treated respectfully. Restaurant owners, caterers, and their teams sincerely want their guests to have a pleasant dining experience. They usually go out of their way to ensure the food, service, and ambience are pleasing. It's inappropriate to make a scene or be demanding or demeaning in a restaurant. If you have concerns about any element of the meal, discreetly ask the server, head waiter, or maître d' to resolve your issues. And always remember to thank the staff for their service.

If you're newlyweds, consider having thank you cards printed at the same time as your invitations, so they are handy for you to send promptly after the wedding. You can also have one of your wedding photographs made into a memorable thank you note following your nuptials. What matters most is that you express your gratitude for people's generosity.

Reciprocity

There's usually no need to feel obligated to invite your host to lunch or dinner after they've treated you to a meal. The choice is yours to make. Most often, a gracious thank you note will suffice. Sometimes, though, you really want to connect with people again. In that case it's fine to say, "I enjoyed our time together so much. Next time, lunch is on me."

Following up with contacts

Whenever you make a commitment to someone during an event, honor it. Always follow up by turning your wishy-washy "shoulds" into definitive "woulds." So, instead of saying, "We *should* get together some day," you'd say, "*Would* you like to get together in the next couple of weeks to continue our conversation?" And then make it happen.

THE ART OF DINING

"

Some of the
most important
conversations I've
ever had occurred
at my family's
dinner table.

Bob Ehrlich

"

HERE IS A DIFFERENCE between eating and dining. We *eat* to survive and, at times, to fill holes in our lives. *Dining*, on the other hand, takes time and involves the perfect combination of flavors, conversation, purpose, and ambience. It can be a highly pleasurable and relaxing activity, and it adds quality to our lives.

When it comes to formal dining skills, you don't know you need them until, well, you find yourself in a position where need them—as I experienced at my first black-tie formal dinner. Yet deals are made, romances are blossomed, friendships are forged, and jobs are landed every day over meals. Knowing about silverware and plates and glasses and linen empowers you to enjoy the company you're with and focus on the subjects at hand, rather than worrying about which fork to use. *Dining is both a social art and a business skill.* Once you understand and master the basics, you'll continue to gain confidence in your personal and professional life.

Gathering around a dining table has a deeper purpose, though. Our current-day "busyness" has resulted in abbreviating everything we do. That includes how we communicate with one another. Taking the time to converse during a meal is, I believe, vital to resuscitate the respect that's lacking in our civility-starved society. For that reason more than any other, I urge you to invite a family member, colleague, neighbor, friend, or even someone you've just met to join you for a meal. Let that person know it's your treat, and then have fun as you share your ideas, discuss your experiences, and energize your hopes and dreams.

> **Whenever we dine together, the flavors of the past mingle with the servings of the present, and the course of the future is held within our hands.**

What The Fork? is more than a book about dining; it's a call to action. This is a critical time for our society; a time for change. And change begins with conversation. Let's sit down with one another over a meal and start talking. Because whenever we dine together, the flavors of the past mingle with the servings of the present, and the course of the future is held within our hands.

Bon Appétit!

ACKNOWLEDGMENTS

"

Be thankful for what you have; you'll end up having more. If you concentrate on what you don't have, you will never, ever have enough.

Oprah Winfrey

"

ACKNOWLEDGMENTS

*T*HIS BOOK IS ENDING where it began— literally. I am writing these words of gratitude in Hawaii, precisely where I entered the Maui Writers Conference a few years ago. Attending that event was the beginning of a magnificent journey of confidence, self-expression, and faith.

It was here I met Sam Horn—author, mentor, speaker, word wizard, and cheerleader. I am sitting within feet of where we first shook hands, a true full-circle moment for me. *Mahalo*, Sam, for your ongoing guidance and support.

Erynn Lyster of Urban Motif Design Inc. is the graphic design genius who has been bringing my visions to life for years. I am grateful for your patience, work ethic, and dedication to this project, Erynn. Thanks for your support and for always making everything look so fabulous!

Editor extraordinaire, Barbara McNichol, casually entered my life in passing in Denver, Colorado. We were serendipitously seated next to one another two years later at a conference in Canada. Somehow she recognized me, and an alliance was forged. Barbara, I am thankful for your professionalism and your extraordinary ability to simplify the syntax.

Sean de Lima is a skilled artist who enthusiastically accepted the challenge of creating the illustrations for this book. Many thanks, Sean. Your drawings add a level of depth and uniqueness that only a visual component can give to a book about dining.

Jessica Jacques Nogueira, a talented professional photographer with a gifted eye and a passion for pictures, eagerly captured my image for the book cover. *Obrigada*, Jess!

My fabulous friends and family, Club Dead sisters, and Springboard mentors have been there every step of the way. Thanks to each of you for your laughter and inspiration over the years. A deep bow goes to you, Bruce Sellery, for your wholehearted encouragement and words of wisdom. And to Ann Marsh, thanks for the memories.

My esteemed colleagues in the world of civility, professionalism, and etiquette are wonderful. I have connected with many of you, worked with some of you, respect all of you, and am grateful to each of you.

Every single *What The Fork?* dining tutorial participant I've had the pleasure of training has added flavor and spice to my career. Thank you for being such good sports as I hovered over your shoulders and watched you dine while I subtly (I hope!) tweaked your body language along the way.

My mom has exhibited down-home hospitality for her whole life—and mine, too. We have shared mealtime laughter with friends, family, and random strangers for as long as I can remember. Thank you, Ruthie, for teaching me how to set a table, put together a decent meal, clean up after myself , and—most importantly—for naturally demonstrating the value of opening the front door for all to enter.

The person who deserves my deepest appreciation is my husband, soul mate, and best friend, Doug. He is the most patient, loving, respectful, and supportive person I have ever met. Fortunately he saw through my uncertainty at that formal dinner all those years ago, and he has held my hand on this entire journey, teaching me about grace, style, confidence, and love along the way. Thank you, Darling. Your belief in me has given me the wings I needed to fly. *Je t'aime!*

ABOUT THE AUTHOR

"
When in doubt,
choose kindness.

Sue Jacques, The Civility CEO®

UE JACQUES IS THE CIVILITY CEO®, a keynote speaker, professionalism coach, and certified etiquette and protocol consultant who specializes in corporate civility. She has been speaking, advising, and writing about professionalism, formal dining, and civility since 2000. Sue has appeared on the Oprah Winfrey Network, Oprah Radio, Business News Network, CTV, CBC, and Global Television.

Before becoming The Civility CEO®, Sue worked for eighteen years as a forensic death investigator at the medical examiners office. During that time she was involved in the medical investigation of thousands of unexpected and often violent deaths, and learned about the ultimate costs of incivility and the value of living fully and authentically.

Sue's mission is to reverse rudeness, revive respect, and create courteous cultures—in homes, businesses, and communities around the world. A former globetrotter and marathon runner, Sue enjoys modeling, music, Muay

Thai, and Maui. She and her husband, a retired funeral director, share countless hours on their boat, which they appropriately named *Life After Death*.

Sue brings enthusiasm and diligence to everything she does. Her personal motto is simple: When in doubt, choose kindness.

To find out more, please visit www.TheCivilityCEO.com